Stardust In My Soil

Kahōkūlani

BookLeaf
Publishing

India | USA | UK

Made with ❤ on the BookLeaf Publishing Platform

www.bookleafpub.in

www.bookleafpub.com

Dedication

To my future self, remember where you have been. Appreciate the experiences, all the highs and lows, and everything in between. The impressions on these pages capture the memories and energy of your past. You've since elevated higher. Protect your evolution as you continue to move in different spaces.

And to those of you hanging in the balance between loving yourself and someone else - choose you, love you. Do not betray yourself for the sake of a relationship. You cannot make one person your everything because that will leave you with nothing for yourself. Pour love back into your soul. Let that love overflow and touch the lives of those around you. The person you are meant to be with will align with you without force and in divine timing.

Preface

A continuation of *You Among the Flowers,* this collection of poetry concludes the journey of "a love that came out of nowhere" and prompted deep self-reflection. It became a catalyst for my growth, forcing me to acknowledge and navigate the unhealed parts of me.

Acknowledgements

Thank you to my family and friends who have continually encouraged me to make space for poetry. We can easily get distracted in life, becoming distant and detached from our passions. I'm blessed to have connections in my circle that remind me of my close relationship to language. The more that I write, the closer I grow to myself.

Cover Design by Tiara Rivera

attuned

i've felt you before
but now i feel closer
i wake up when you do
although i'm not supposed to

you've got the sun
while i see the moon
even with the vastness of space
we remain attuned

my heart hurts when yours does
i feel my body change
we cry at the same time
and i experience all your pain

there are moments when i miss you
it's part of the human condition
but you're never too far
call it intuition

but we're spiritually entwined
deeper than others can see
it goes beyond the basic understanding
of a lover's decree

a statement of tenderness doesn't seem enough
to explain all that we feel and think
and what we'd do for the other to be happy
while moving forward in sync

i don't think i entirely understand
why this feels so intense
it happened so suddenly, out of nowhere
sometimes it doesn't make sense

but i revel in all that we are
i wouldn't change a thing
i could never take a moment back
i own every feeling

weekend memory

not much time has passed since i saw you
but it feels like a distant memory
of us sharing breath
and exposing vulnerability

i'm in awe that you're real
not just a voice over the phone
more than a picture or text
a soul matched to my own

i don't know what's going to happen
i'm not sure what meeting you means
where do we go from here?
there are endless possibilities

the only outcome i desire
is something you're not willing to do
you tell me you're not ready
and that i'm too far away from you

and i know you're not always willing to talk
about past hurt you've been through
there's layers of shame and fear
the thought it will be heavy on me too

we're all dragged down and haunted
and sometimes it's hard to face it alone
i'm here, it's safe to open your eyes
you don't have to fight the world on your own

come find me when you're ready
until then i'll watch our lives unfold
while i think of our weekend fondly
and release the idea of control

grief

you stopped forever
before it began
unable to carry love
with this knife through my hand

my spirit bleeds
it's pooling all over the floor
i'm wandering and lost
the world collapses beyond the door

everything is ruined
all the flowers are dead
the flame is blown out
my heart obliterated

my soul feels it too
it's detaching from my body
it's home no longer warm
when there's no one to love me

every face of trauma appeared
now you're just one of them
another person to hurt me
casted away, abandoned

you think you're saving me in the end
to cry about it now, rather than later
you pushed me away and lied
i don't know which pain is greater

tears endlessly escaping
there's no moment of peace
i'm just numb now
my eyes defaulted to grief

i see your messages
if i reply, i won't stand a chance
it will continually break me
your words won't fill your absence

you will never be here the way i need you to be
the way that i want
you're limited in your capacity
i need more than just your thoughts

what is there even to say at this point?
you've made your decision
there's nothing here for me
i need to adjust my vision

chaos

there's no escaping the snapshots
the memories are invasive
if i'm to drown in these thoughts
i'll bury you in pages

can you feel the magnitude of my emotions?
have i illustrated enough?
depths greater than the oceans
and i'm just at the cusp

warning to the love of a creative:
you can be painted as the greatest design
or your character can be debated
in a single poetic line

you can't change what you started
there's no reshaping the shrub
i'm left stranded in your garden
knee deep in the mud

but i'll find my strength again
soon as these feelings subside
keep the love i've given
i can't pack it back inside

there's no use in trying to soothe me
no actions to undo
my feelings are wild, unruly
let the chaos ensue

sacred

i'm not here for aimless affection
i'm sacred
it will take a profound connection
to bare my soul naked

i'm a goddess you see
emanating beauty from the inside
if it's just a body you seek
then it is you i have to decline

i'm no ordinary lover
no random you find in bed
you'll need to spend time to uncover
the thoughts i bury in my head

all the secrets i keep hidden
even from myself
digging deep into the forbidden
shadows on the shelf

it's a massive library
of books never seen
endless pages of commentary
the burdens of a queen

you will have to be patient
you can't check them all out at once
there might be some complications
just give me time to adjust

i'm worth the read
to discover the unknown and
your soul will be the key
to unlock the unopened

introspection

time for solitude
i've been here before
releasing old energy
from deep within my core

contemplating my actions
making space for self-reflection
i need this period of shedding
taking time for introspection

why do i allow you
to affect me so intensely?
why do i act out of bounds
and feel everything so immensely?

i've given you this power
to control the way my blood flows
all of my limbs go numb
my body wants to implode

i have too many thoughts
and i always overthink
searching for more meaning
i ruminate until i sleep

i need to let go of my expectations
rise above the human condition
to master my body again
and take back your permission

misery

i can't fight the misery inside me
i just want to let it go
although it fuels my writing
my death is painfully slow

i find myself catastrophizing
thinking of the worst
my world crumbles now that i'm recognizing
the gravity of this hurt

grasping whatever reasoning i can
to keep me on the ground
if i float too high, there's nowhere to land
but if i'm too low i might drown

nobody wants to hear they're unwanted
how do you even move forward?
we chase as if we can stop them
from whatever they're moving toward

i have to let my grip go to be free
maybe it's poor timing
there i go again thinking logically
so misery comes back and finds me

fantasy

i've relinquished the illusion
that i had any control
i filtered through my confusion
of what i thought would make me whole

you can't make me happy
i won't allow you access
nobody deserves that authority
it will just take me practice

to dedicate to things
that will fill my cup
i'll undo my suffering
and not give up

all that belongs to me will align
because i'm operating from my heart space
it will get better in time
everything will fall into the right place

i got caught up in a fantasy
a novel that i authored
it's a love and lesson for me
for a title never offered

i no longer want to dwell
on what could have been
i'll revert back to before i fell
and rewrite the pages within

oblivion

although i'd like to revel
in love and all its glory
i want to release this feeling
rid myself of what i'm storing

i know it won't happen
i'm too emotionally invested
my soul belongs with yours
it's impossible to be disconnected

and i find myself still longing
for a grand gesture of romance
an action that says, "i love you,"
that you'd like to give us a chance

oh, the mind of a romantic
i want this dream to drift into oblivion
to accept what you're not to me
because that's the reality i'm living in

detour

drudging through the viscosity of my thoughts
my emotions are thick
i can't see past what i feel
i'm too mal-equipped

to handle what i'm experiencing
and be considerate of you
i am self-centered, the victim
although you're hurting too

but i'm not thinking about your heart
or if i should comfort you
in the moment i don't care to check in
or to understand your point of view

i need time to process my loss
yes, you're here, but i want more
i want you in every way beyond a friend
is this just a detour?

is this just an alternate path?
should i still hold onto the idea?
but i would be blocking my blessings
while this remains confusing and unclear

i can't keep hoping to have you
i need to let go and be done
because if i hold on too tightly
you'll just continue to run

to fall in love with you

you can't imagine what it's like
when your body doesn't feel like your own
i've completely lost control
because my love for you has grown

my thoughts are flooded wondering if you're safe
if you've eaten enough, if you've had a good day
i wait to hear from you all night
hoping that you're sleeping okay

i'm concerned about your peace
if your heart is full
i pray your innermost thoughts don't betray you
that you're fulfilled and whole

my heart doesn't listen to me
it's eager to pursue
i tell myself i need to let you go
but it's stubborn and only asks for you

my stomach drops when i see you
tingling sensations when i hear your voice
my cravings pulsate from below
i feel all of this with no choice

i see you in my dreams
is it a past life or somewhere down the line?
speaking it into reality
asking my cards for a sign

you can't imagine what it's like
to box and keep hidden
what it is i truly want
this desire not given

in the end

why do we have such capacity
to hurt one another?
why does it feel like tragedy
in the absence of the other?

is this actually toxic
or is this healing?
i feel compelled to fix it
to stop this internal bleeding

i feel like an empty cavity
but also full of pain
can't understand what's happening
is love sick a thing?

if i really didn't care
i'd pay this no mind
my heart would be easy to spare
and move on in no time

but this connection is rare
a match from the divine
others fail to compare
when you and i are aligned

somehow in the end
we come back together
our bond never broken
and inseparable tether

complicated

we tip toe on the sidelines
sometimes crossing over
to do what lovers do

then i need to rewind
thinking what i told her
knowing i need to regroup

never regretting those times
knowing what we were
there's nothing more i could do

obsessing in my mind
and wanting to be sure
there's nothing left to pursue

emotional landscape

why would the universe send me someone
i can't have?
when she can be anything for me
except that?

i'm scraping a concrete wall
with a plastic spoon
hoping the smallest effort
would grant me a view

she's barricaded herself so deep
she forgot the way out
seemingly endless labyrinth of
flowers and thorns – one thousand routes

will i ever find that one?
that one that leads me to her center?
where the candle light flickers
where the torment had left her

i see traces of her all around
picking up the small pieces she leaves behind
tucking them deep into my pocket
for safe keeping as if they're mine

guarding her secrets and chasing her shadow
i follow her damaged silhouette
but the closer i get, the further she burrows
because her running never ends

she's scared to feel the letdown, the pain
that she'll lose sight of her being
questioning if i can accept the stains
if her truth is even worth seeing

so how do i show her when words
don't hold weight?
and if i roll up my sleeves, to reveal my scars
will that muddy the space?

will she hide her eyes and disappear on me?
leaving me in my emotional landscape
then all that i've done will lose its meaning
forced to watch my failures take shape

but all of this is anxiety and fear
our hearts know that this is real
the depth of our connection is abundantly clear
and we can help each other move on and heal

the day you pave that road for me
i will happily walk it
and when i'm brave enough to open my door
there's no going back to lock it

the cycle

i listen to those songs when i miss you
because somehow i feel closer
i meet you in my dreams
and it's there that i am chosen

it's a tease of my desire
and with the first sight of the ceiling
i let out a depressed exhalation
there are no words for this feeling

you're encased in the bronze of a locket
a vintage trinket nearly within my grasp
waiting for the right time to unlock it
to behold all the value behind its clasp

feeling ship wrecked and lost at times
when the waves become too great
panic like water in my lungs
and i begin to suffocate

choking on words and thoughts
of the sensations of your touch
hope is stagnant and rots
i give up because it's too much

when the cycle is complete
somehow i fall even deeper
you command my heart's fleet
am i to be your lock keeper?

i take to battle my emotions
with an arsenal of skills
you anchor me in this ocean
and bring down all my shields

and you remain there unmoved
because it is always me who travels
you wait for me to return home
after i've unraveled

you let me storm until the rain lifts
even though you're *mi tormenta*
i can't drift too far away
because i'm always called back to the center

existence

i exist in between the lines
in the creases of thoughts and words
in the space between my rhymes
each adjective and verb

you can find me in the color of obscurity
or in the dark of explicit emotion
i'm peering from the edge of clarity
and i set the metric in motion

i'm the beginning, end
the story at its peak
i'm the smile on your face
and the tear down your cheek

you're engulfed in the flame of my passion
i am there as you melt
you see as i see
i'm everything that you felt

you can fall in love with her too
with the way she is written
i author a love you can marvel
with the talent i was gifted

you'll discover yourself
as i provoke you to think
you sense me on every page
i'm the dried-up ink

i'm in the fantasy you envision
when you read these verses
you can find me in unlocked memories
and the experience you're immersed in

and when my physical body rests on command
my words will echo on
just imagine me with a pen in my hand
in the creative space that i belong

another lesson

i'm mentally exhausted
and emotionally spent
stable footing – i lost it
is this what it is to lament?

at what point will you not affect me?
when will i stop being triggered?
another lesson to love unconditionally
to give you space and not be bitter

because it's not about me
but my inner child is wounded
there's still need for healing
for something so deeply rooted

maybe i need a break too
to sift through these thoughts
because it's also not about you
this is a bridge i need to cross

it's an endless journey
of repairing this damage
i'm constantly learning
and it's getting easier to manage

i'm deepening my understanding
of how i process hurt
i replenish the energy it's demanding
for all that i need to unearth

i know i require a lot of patience
there are very few who have it
it can make for difficult relations
to filter through the havoc

and at the end of the day
you reflect what i need to mend
all of the internal disarray
that needs order before i transcend

vines

it's okay to unravel your vines
it's safe to emerge from your cocoon
you can let all the green unwind
i'll collect the flowers you have bloomed

i'll help keep them blossoming
as you remain the sun
it's growth that i'm promising
my moonlight they can't outrun

you shine over our fields
i keep moisture in the soil
the foundation needs us both to heal
in time all the weeds will foil

we move and feel as one
although at times we are day and night
we circle back to where we've begun
when our system settles and everything's right

we can walk endlessly in this energetic garden
and we can never separate completely
even if the world around us hardens
we dance in this space freely

your vines have safeguarded you over time
and not just anyone can get past them
not everyone is deserving of that climb
not everyone is meant to ascend

but who am i to think that i am worthy?
maybe it's more of a feeling, a knowing
because what would our world be
if this garden wasn't worth growing?

we move forward together compassionately
it's what our journey needs
the sun pairs with the moon naturally
they both nourish the seeds

so when your vines finally loosen their grip
and you take that step outward
i know i'll be ready and equipped
to tend to all your flowers

watered down

watering my own roots with my tears
hoping i would hurry and bloom
but peace is farther than it appears
because i have so much growth to do

i need to dig deeper
and parent "little me"
i've done too much self-neglecting
out of concern for your liberty

i hand you carefully arranged bouquets
even if the prickles cause me to bleed
i would lay in a bed of thorns
if that gives you what you need

but now it's time to shift inward
and pull out all of the weeds
cultivate my own grounds
instead of what's outside of me

but don't be afraid to ask for a tool or two
i could never leave you empty-handed
you can find me in my garden
i'm here as i always have been

dandelion

laying in a field
my back against the grass
watching clouds shift in slow motion
appearing as people from my past

i sigh and turn over
can you imagine what i see?
a gathering of thriving dandelions
although some call them weeds

they may be invasive
sometimes growing out of control
very much like what's inside of me
pandemonium without lull

if only it was as easy
to detach from what fatigues
as it is when you blow away
a dandelion's seeds

i can still feel my disgust
the hot breath and touch
i'm chained to these moments
the weight is too much

but i'm in there somewhere
beneath the filth and cruelty
while dandelions can still be beautiful
even if they're not always thought to be

stardust in my soil

elevating with each breath i take
i give love where it is deserved
serving my life's purpose
my inner child finally mothered

when i'm unconditional to myself
it reflects back to you
your awareness shifts with mine
do you feel that gravitational pull?

the actions that we take
to illuminate the shadows
bring stillness to all the ripples
in our mind's meadows

those memories floating on the water's surface
mirror where we've been
but they will no longer drown us
from there we've only strengthened

we walk along different graveled paths
but on the same journey
the sun's radiance leads your way
as the moonlight shows me

eventually we will find peace
there will be more smiles than tears
we will reclaim the parts of us
that we lost along the years

you will bask under the rays
blossoming from the turmoil
and my garden will be lustrous on the moon
with stardust in my soil